SPORTS BIOGRAPHIES

SHAUN WHITE

KENNY ABDO

Fly!
An Imprint of Abdo Zoom
abdobooks.com

abdobooks.com

Published by Abdo Zoom, a division of ABDO, P.O. Box 398166, Minneapolis, Minnesota 55439. Copyright © 2023 by Abdo Consulting Group, Inc. International copyrights reserved in all countries. No part of this book may be reproduced in any form without written permission from the publisher. Fly!™ is a trademark and logo of Abdo Zoom.

Printed in the United States of America, North Mankato, Minnesota.
102022
012023

Photo Credits: AP Images, Getty Images, iStock, Shutterstock
Production Contributors: Kenny Abdo, Jennie Forsberg, Grace Hansen
Design Contributors: Neil Klinepier

Library of Congress Control Number: 2022937317

Publisher's Cataloging-in-Publication Data

Names: Abdo, Kenny, author.
Title: Shaun White / by Kenny Abdo
Description: Minneapolis, Minnesota : Abdo Zoom, 2023 | Series: Sports biographies | Includes online resources and index.
Identifiers: ISBN 9781098280291 (lib. bdg.) | ISBN 9781098280826 (ebook) | ISBN 9781098281120 (Read-to-Me ebook)
Subjects: LCSH: White, Shaun, 1986---Juvenile literature. | Olympic athletes--Juvenile literature. | Winter Olympics--Juvenile literature. | Snowboarders--Juvenile literature.
Classification: DDC 796.092--dc23

TABLE OF CONTENTS

Shaun White 4

Early Years...................... 8

Going Pro...................... 12

Legacy 18

Glossary 22

Online Resources 23

Index 24

SHAUN WHITE

4

Known for his flowing red hair and amazing feats on the half-pipe, Shaun White is one of the coolest figures in snowboarding history!

Nicknamed "the Flying Tomato," White burst onto the **Olympic** stage in 2006, collecting three gold medals throughout his exciting career!

EARLY YEARS

Shaun Roger White was born in San Diego, California, in 1986. He was surrounded by surfing, skateboarding, and snowboarding, which lead to his passion for the sports.

White had heart problems when he was just a baby. He needed two operations before the age of one. By the age of five, he was hitting the **slopes** and skate parks!

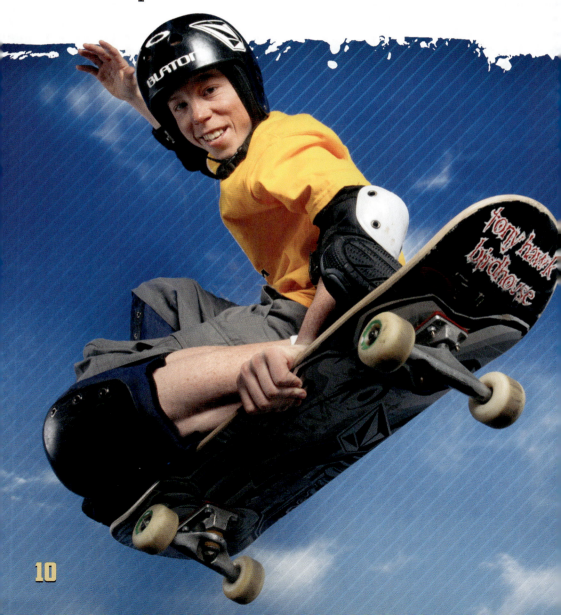

White won his first snowboarding competition at just seven years old! White turned professional at age 13 and made his **debut** at the Winter **X Games** in 2000.

GOING PRO

White won his first **Olympic** gold medal at the 2006 Torino Games. He nabbed another gold medal at the 2010 Vancouver Olympics!

White was the first athlete to compete in both the Winter and Summer **X Games**. By 2011, he had won five gold medals in **slopestyle**. He also has two gold medals in skateboarding!

While training in 2017, White suffered a nasty crash. **Bailing** on a double flip **1440**, he face-planted. It resulted in more than 60 stitches.

White still participated in the 2018 Pyeongchang Games. He won the gold medal in the halfpipe. White became the first snowboarder to win three **Olympic** gold medals!

White took on his fifth **Olympic** halfpipe event at the 2022 Beijing Games. After placing fourth, he announced that he was retiring from the sport.

LEGACY

SHAUN WHITE
BEST OLYMPIC MOMENT

Because of his success on the **slopes**, White has won 10 **ESPY** awards in his career. He was also featured in *Forbes'* "30 under 30" in 2016!

White changed the sport for future generations to come. Holding the world record for most **X Games** and **Olympic** gold medals by a snowboarder, he shreds more than just the **gnar**!

GLOSSARY

1440 – a snowboard trick with four full rotations.

bail – to purposely quit midway through a trick and fall.

debut – a first appearance.

ESPY – short for "Excellence in Sports Performance Yearly," the award is given to an athlete or team that did the best in their event that year.

gnar – short for "gnarly," used to describe the terrain that is snowboarded on. "Shredding the gnar" is a popular term heard on the slopes.

Olympic Games – the biggest international athletic event held as separate winter and summer competitions every four years in a different city.

slope – either a snow-covered mountain or man-made structure which you can snowboard down.

slopestyle – a discipline of freestyle snowboarding involving an obstacle course.

X Games – an extreme sports competition that is held twice a year. There is a summer and a winter competition.

ONLINE RESOURCES

To learn more about Shaun White, please visit **abdobooklinks.com** or scan this QR code. These links are routinely monitored and updated to provide the most current information available.

INDEX

California 9

ESPY Awards 18

Forbes (magazine) 18

health 10, 15

injury 15

medals 12, 14

Olympics 7, 12, 16, 17, 21

retirement 17

skateboarding 10, 14

X Games 11, 14, 21